LONGMAN

INSIGHTS *into* BUSINESS

WORKBOOK

GRAHAM TULLIS

MICHAEL LANNON

Addison Wesley Longman Limited
Edinburgh Gate
Harlow
Essex
CM20 2JE
England
and Associated Companies throughout the world.

Acknowledgements

The authors would like to thank the following for their help:

Michel Carnelez, Cooper Tools: Jean-Louis Barsoux, INSEAD; Asea Brown Boveri Ltd.; Imagine That!!!; Scott D. Reames, Nike, Inc.; First Direct; Andrew Currie, Isle of Arran Distillers; Frank Kindred, BT.

The publishers would like to thank the following for their kind permission to use their material in this book:

Cooper Tools, p.1; Reed Business Publishing, p.8; Swatch Watches, p.10; Avery Publishing Group, Inc. for material adapted from *Taking Charge: Making the Right Choices* by Perry M. Smith, © 1993, 1988, p.12; *The World in 1992*, p.15; African Wildlife Foundation, p.16; Advertising Standards Authority, p.19; Ben & Jerry's, p.20; Imagine That!!!, p.22; *BLOOMBERG Business News*, p.24; B & Q, p.28; *Independent on Sunday*, p.31; Richer Sounds plc, p.34; Volvo, p.44; *The European*, p.44; *International Herald Tribune*, p.48; Isle of Arran Distillers, p.51; BT, pp.60, 62; *Financial Times*, p.63.

Photographs:

The Advertising Archives p.10; J. Allan Cash, p.36; Rex Features Limited pp.24, 42, 60; The Telegraph Colour Library pp.6, 16; Zefa Picture Library p.11.

Illustrations:

Mike Kenny, p.15; Neil John Macmillan, p.19 (Spanish villa); Michael Roscoe, p.31. Other illustrations by Dan Feldon and Judy Allen-Storey.

Design by Aricot Vert.

The publishers have made every effort to contact owners of copyright, but this has not been possible in all cases. They apologise for any omissions, and if details are sent, will be glad to rectify these when the title is reprinted.

Contents

Company Structures

READING   Look at the organisation chart for Cooper France. Where should the following labels appear?

general manager	**sales manager**	**sales representative**
sales secretary	**agent**	

Now read the passage and complete the chart to show the positions that Jean Lamadon and his colleagues occupy.

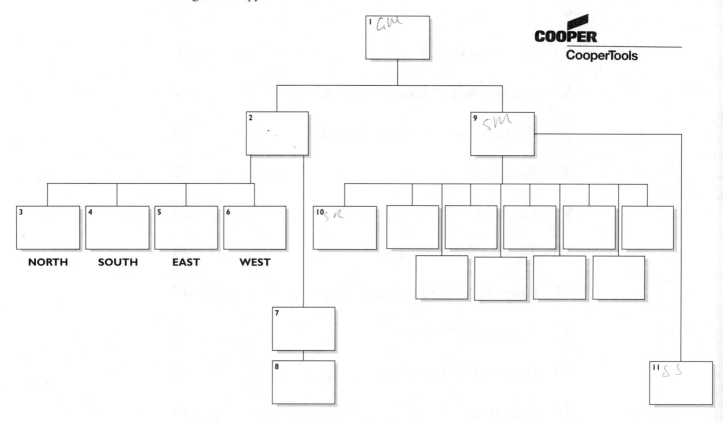

> My name's Jean Lamadon, and I'm one of the two sales managers here at Cooper France. Cooper is an international group based in America which, among other things, produces tools and equipment for the professional and consumer markets. The group has subsidiaries in several European countries.
>
> I suppose that if I'm going to describe how things are organised here in France I'd better start at the top! That's where you'll find Alain Madrange who is everybody's boss here! He controls all aspects of finance and is in permanent contact with our head office. Both myself and Michel Carnelez, who is the other sales manager, report directly to him.

As I said, there are two sales managers, because we sell two very different categories of product in France. The first is electrical equipment which is used for assembling components for printed circuit boards. That's my area. The other is what we call 'tools and hardware' which includes a lot of quite different products, mostly sold in Do-It-Yourself shops all over the country. Michel Carnelez is in charge of that, and he doesn't have any Cooper employees working under him apart from Sylvie Cieutat, his sales secretary. That means he relies entirely on a national network of ten sales agents including his Paris agent Daniel Royatte. Michel spends much more time than I do marketing and promoting his products.

The way my department is organised is really quite simple. About 80% of our business is done through distributors and the rest is direct to major account holders, who are our really big customers. As we sell all over the country this means I need a team of sales people. At the moment there are four, each responsible for one territory: Cyril Jehanne for the north, Jean-Noël Echave for the south, Daniel Lorand for the west and Patrick Amat for the east. I also have a customer services assistant, Jocylène Cuisy, and a sales secretary, Marie-Christine Chaussadas. Together they run the sales office and look after most of the administration. 9

VOCABULARY

1 Circle the word that does not belong in each horizontal group.

1 business	company	society	subsidiary
2 salary	manager	salesman	employee
3 finance	product	research	marketing
4 distributing	selling	assembling	promoting
5 components	tools	hardware	strategy
6 end user	customer	client	distributor

2 Which of the groups of three words that you identified above refer to the following definitions?

a people who buy goods or services   ....

b types of commercial organisations   ....

c different departments or functions   ....

d people who work inside a company   ....

e activities that involve meeting customers..

f products that can be sold   ....

3 Match each of the words that you circled with the following:

1 .... a monthly payment in exchange for work

2 .... an item that has been made

3 .... a plan of action

4 .... a non-profit-making organisation

5 .... putting parts together

6 .... a person or business which has an agreement to sell the goods of another firm

Present perfect and past simple

Read the short profile below of Dimmen Herwarden, a manager with a major American consumer products company.

CURRICULUM VITAE

Name	Dimmen Herwarden
Nationality	Dutch
Age	39
Marital Status	Married Kate Taylor in 1980 No children
Civil Status	Permanent resident from 1980 Working visa 1978-1980 Student visa 1975-1977
Qualifications	MBA Columbia University 1977 Dutch high school leaving certificate 1974

Employment		
	1982 to date:	Taylor Corporation
	1979-1981:	ESPV Inc.
	1978-1979:	Research Systems Inc.

Positions held with current employer		
	1992 to date:	General Manager
	1987-1991:	Brand Manager
	1984-1986:	Assistant Brand Manager
	1982-1983:	Brand assistant

Present perfect

With the present perfect we use *How long...?* for questions about duration and *for* or *since* for the answer (you may wish to refer to the grammar notes on page 153 of the Students' Book):

How long have you been a permanent resident?
I've been a permanent resident since 1980.

Past simple

With the past simple we use *When...?* and *How long...?* to ask questions about the timing and duration of events in the past:

When did you come to the States? (TIMING)
How long did you live in Holland? (DURATION)

We can answer the first question by giving the exact time in the past or by giving the total number of units of time that separate the event from the present:

I came in 1975.
I came 19 years ago.

Question two can only be answered by giving the duration of the event:

*I lived in Holland **for 23 years/from 1955 to 1978**.*

Using the present perfect or the past simple where appropriate, write five questions about the timing and duration of the following things in Mr Herwarden's life.

1 Marriage ....

2 First job ....

3 Present position ....

4 MBA ....

5 The Taylor Corporation ....

Now refer back to the notes about Mr Herwarden and write in the answer to each of your questions.

a ....

b ....

c ....

d ....

e ....

WRITING Write a short company profile of ABB using the information below. Show how the company is organised and how it has performed in its different markets.

NAME OF COMPANY
ABB (Asea Brown Boveri Ltd.)
HEADQUARTERS
Zurich, Switzerland
CHAIRMAN
Percy Barnevik
EMPLOYEES WORLDWIDE
213, 407
TOTAL REVENUES, 1992:
US $ 29.6 Billion

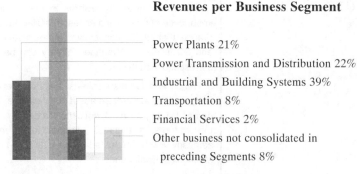

Revenues per Business Segment

Power Plants 21%

Power Transmission and Distribution 22%

Industrial and Building Systems 39%

Transportation 8%

Financial Services 2%

Other business not consolidated in
  preceding Segments 8%

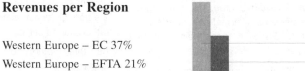

Revenues per Region

Western Europe – EC 37%

Western Europe – EFTA 21%

North America NAFTA 17%

Asia and Australasia 17%

Africa, East Europe,
  South America 8%

Employees per Region

Western Europe – EC 37%

Western Europe – EFTA 28%

North America 14%

Asia and Australasia 10%

Africa, East Europe,
  South America 11%

EFTA = European Free Trade Association
NAFTA = North American Free Trade Association

Source: 1993 Annual Report

Recruitment

READING

Read the following text which explains how job advertisements differ in three European countries.

JOB ADS:
READING BETWEEN THE LINES

Checking out job advertisements is popular with executives worldwide. But though the activity is universal, is the same true of the advertisements? Are executive positions in different countries advertised in the same way? A comparison of the jobs pages of *The Times* of London, *Le Monde* of Paris and Germany's *Frankfurter Allgemeine Zeitung* suggests not.

First, what UK job seekers consider an essential piece of information – what the post pays – is absent from French and German adverts. It is often left to applicants to raise this themselves. In contrast, most British advertisements mention not only salary, but also other material incentives including a car and fringe benefits. French or German advertisements rarely refer to these.

The attention given to rewards in the UK indicates the importance of the job and its responsibility. In Germany and France, that information is given by the level of experience and qualifications demanded. Salary can be assumed to correspond with this.

If French and German adverts are vague about material rewards, they are precise about qualifications. They usually demand 'a degree in....', not simply 'a degree'. In Germany, for example, a technical director for a machine tool company will be expected to have a *Dipl.-Ing* degree in Mechanical Engineering.

French advertisements go further. They may specify not just the type of *grande école* degree, but sometimes a particular set of institutions *(Formation supérieure X, Centrale, Mines, HEC, ESSEC)*, these being the most famous *grandes écoles*.

All this contrasts with the vague call for 'graduates' (or 'graduate preferred') which is found in the UK. British companies often give the impression that they have a particular type of applicant in mind, but are not sure about the supply and will consider others. Their wording suggests hope and uncertainty, as in this advertisement from

The Times: 'Whilst educational standards are obviously important, a large measure of personal oomph* is likely to secure the success of your application.'

In the UK qualifications beyond degree level make employers nervous, but in France or Germany it is difficult to be 'overqualified'. Many people on German executive boards have doctorates and the French regard five or six years of intensive post-*baccalauréat* study at a *grande école* as ideal training. British managers are not selected primarily for their intelligence, as managers are in France, or for their expert knowledge, as in Germany. Instead, the British give importance to social, political and leadership skills.

This difference also shows in the personal qualities mentioned. British advertisements stress energy, ability to communicate and motivate. German advertisements like achievement, but it tends to be less personality-driven. German companies want candidates with sound knowledge, experience and competence in their field. They rarely recruit novices as do British employers. French advertisements refer more to intellectual qualities like analytical aptitude and independence.

Even the tone of the job advertisements is different in the three countries. By French and German standards, British advertisements are very racy**: They attract young executives with challenges such as: 'Are you reaching your potential?', whereas French and German advertisements are boringly direct, aiming to give information about the job rather than to sell it.

All this points to three different conceptions of management. The French regard it as intellectually complex, the Germans as technically complex, and the British as interpersonally complex. But they agree on one thing: it's complex. *Jean-Louis Barsoux*

MAY 1993 INTERNATIONAL MANAGEMENT *(adapted)*

* *oomph = enthusiasm* ** *racy = bold, audacious*

Now complete the chart with the information each country provides in its advertisements.

	UK	FRANCE	GERMANY
SALARY	*Essential piece of information.*	*Not mentioned; applicant expected to give details of anticipated salary.*	*Same as France.*
MATERIAL INCENTIVES	car, fringe benefits	—	—
DEGREES/QUALIFICATIONS	a degree	a degree i	
SCHOOL ATTENDED	X	✓	not given.
PERSONAL QUALITIES			
TONE OF JOB ADVERTISEMENT			
CONCEPTIONS OF MANAGEMENT			

VOCABULARY   1 Prefixes

Look at the following sentences taken from the text on page 16 of the Students' Book:

*There is something downright **undemocratic** about judging managers' abilities ...* (lines 1-2)

*In some case, **unhappy** employees are challenging the arbitrary rules ...* (lines 14-15)

Notice than in both examples, the prefix *un-* gives an opposite and negative meaning to the adjectives democratic and happy. There are several prefixes in English which have the same function; *dis-, il-, im-, in-, ir-, un-*. Add a prefix to the adjectives below to give each an opposite meaning. You may need a dictionary to help you.

1	relevant experience	*irrelevant experience*	10	a loyal employee	....
2	a complete CV	....	11	an effective letter of application	....
3	a fair decision	....	12	sufficient training	....
4	a popular manager	....	13	an equal salary	....
5	a responsible worker	....	14	perfect skills	....
6	satisfied staff	....	15	a qualified candidate	....
7	an expected promotion	....	16	a logical argument	....
8	an honest character	....			
9	a competent engineer	....			

2 Job advertisement

1 Use the job advertisements on pages 14 and 18 of the Students' Book to help you to complete the advert below with words from the list.

competitive	.... *h*	plus	....
degree	....	resources	....
experienced	....	responsibility	....
manager	....	successful	....
market	....		

2 Do you know what Swatch's logo is also the graphic symbol of?

....

3 Which expression in the advertisement means that the company employs people regardless of their sex, race or religion?

....

4 Using the following words from the advertisement, write five sentences which might appear in an advertisement for the job you do or would like to do.

confidential	opportunity	candidate
comprehensive		key

....
....
....
....
....
....
....
....
....

swatch

Be an important part of our winning team! We are presently seeking __a__ *sales professionals who are*

- Dedicated, - Dynamic,
- Professional, - Energetic.

MARKETING __b__

__c__ candidate will develop and execute overall marketing strategy, work with key accounts and take hands-on __d__ for small profit centre. Qualified candidates must have 5+ years' sales/marketing experience dealing with this kind of __e__. BA __f__ in marketing and familiarity with children's market a __g__.

We offer __h__ compensation and a comprehensive benefits package.

For consideration, please send confidential resume with sales history to:

Ms. Clarke, Human __i__

SMH (US) Inc.

35 East 21st St., New York, N.Y. 10010.

An equal opportunity employer

LANGUAGE FOCUS

Present simple and present continuous

Read the interview with Philippe André, a French executive. Put the verbs in brackets in the present simple or the present continuous tense.

'I [1] _____work_____ (work) for Techno Profile, a medium-sized company just outside Paris, selling and manufacturing electronic components for different applications. I [2] _____ (be) the finance manager which [3] _____ (mean) that I [4] _____ (have) complete responsibility for all aspects of our financial policy. I carefully [5] _____ (follow) the results of our six regional offices in France. This year the company [6] _____ (introduce) a new range of products that we [7] _____ (import) from Germany. Next week I [8] _____ (go) to Bordeaux to meet the office manager and discuss developments in the south-west region. At the moment I [9] _____ (make) about 28,000 Francs a month with a bonus which, of course, [10] _____ (depend) on results. I [11] _____ (live) in a large apartment in the centre of town and [12] _____ (drive) to work every day in the company car. I [13] _____ (get) five weeks paid holiday a year which I usually [14] _____ (spend) in Spain with my wife and kids.'

WRITING

Using the given introduction, write a short job advertisement for publication in a British newspaper. Do not forget to mention salary, benefits, job location and a description of the job (Regional Marketing Manager for a range of interactive video games). Remember that the purpose of the advertisement is to attract as many suitable candidates as possible.

'You're a recent graduate and you're successful. Now ask yourself this question. Is it enough?'

Management Styles

READING   Read the pieces of advice, in paragraphs 1-9, to leaders within different types of organisations. Then choose the appropriate heading for each from the list below.

a   A leader should be a good teacher and communicator. .... *5* ....

b   A leader must manage time and use it effectively. ....

c   A leader must have technical competence. ....

d   A leader must provide vision. ....

e   A leader must be visible and approachable. ....

f   Leaders should be introspective. ....

g   Leaders should be dependable. ....

h   Leaders should be open-minded. ....

i   Leaders should have a sense of humour. ....

1   In large organisations, leaders should spend no more than four hours a day in their offices. The rest of the time, they should be out with their people, talking to lower - level employees and getting their feedback on problem areas. They should be making short speeches and handing out awards. They should be travelling widely throughout their organisations.

2   The best leaders are those whose minds are never closed and who are eager to deal with new issues. Leaders should not change their minds too frequently after a major decision has been made, but if they never reconsider, they are beginning to show a degree of rigidity and inflexibility that creates problems for the organisation.

3   Executives must discipline their schedules, their post, their telephones, their travel schedules and their meetings. Staying busy and working long hours are not necessarily a measurement of leadership effectiveness.

4   Leaders may run efficient organisations, but they do not really serve the long-term interests of the institution unless they plan, set goals and provide strategic perception.

5   The leader must be willing to teach skills, to share insights and experiences, and to work very closely with people to help them mature and be creative.

6   Leaders should let people know that life is not so important that you can't sit back occasionally and be amused by what is happening. Humour can be a great reliever of tension.

7 Reliability is something that leaders must have in order to provide stability and strength to organisations. Leaders must be willing to be flexible but consistency and coherence are important elements of large organisations.

8 Leaders must not only understand the major elements of their businesses but also must keep up with the changes.

9 Leaders should be able to look at themselves objectively and analyse where they have made mistakes and where they have disappointed people.

VOCABULARY Review the words from the key vocabulary section (pages 24-25) as well as from the text (page 26) of the Students' Book. Use the word 'management' and the clues provided to complete the grid below.

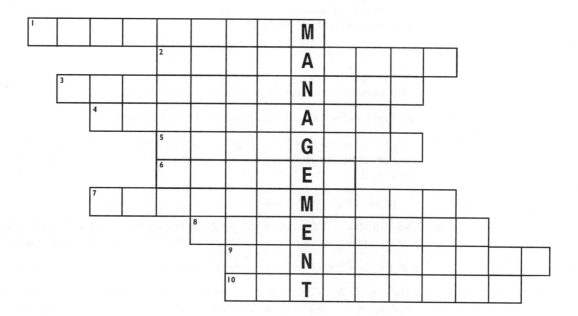

1 A negative judgement of something or somebody.

2 The different levels of a company.

3 A person who works under you.

4 We say that employees are made .... when they lose their jobs for economic reasons.

5 To share responsibilities, to let others take decisions.

6 A person who motivates others and helps them to reach a common goal.

7 The way a person does his or her job; it can be measured.

8 Money or other benefits given in addition to a salary.

9 The introduction of new ideas; creativity.

10 The right to take decisions and give orders.

LANGUAGE FOCUS

1 Adjectives of Nationality

Read the ten short passages. Below each one you will find a sentence which you should complete, using an adjective of nationality. Make sure that your sentences reflect the information that is contained in the passage itself.

1 Packard Bell Electronics has already taken 10% of the US computer market and has performed better, in some areas, than its two main national rivals Compaq and Apple.

Compaq, Apple and Packard bell are .... *American* ....

2 Nordak is currently recruiting a senior manager who will head up the UK office of its first foreign subsidiary.

Nordak is not of .... origin.

3 The shares of Heineken NV reached a record level of 244.5 guilders yesterday on their home market in Amsterdam, Holland.

Heineken is a .... company.

4 The 'Société de Bourse Française' publishes an annual guide to the 120 biggest national companies whose shares are sold on the Paris exchange.

The Paris exchange sells the shares of the 120 biggest .... companies.

5 Coroll have received several enquiries from companies who are interested in representing their products in Spain. However, for the time being they have no intention of expanding into this part of Europe.

Coroll has no plans to enter the .... market.

6 The Ministry of Trade and Industry in Japan has for the first time awarded licences to six foreign firms who can now operate investment funds on the Tokyo market.

The Tokyo market was previously restricted to .... firms.

7 This year we have decided not to attend the 'Fiera Milan' trade fair in Italy as the date coincides with a similar but more important event in Frankfurt in Germany.

We will be attending the .... trade fair.

8 Our main markets are Eastern Europe and North America. However, we also do some business with Portugal.

The .... market is not one of our most important.

9 Whenever we set up a foreign subsidiary, we always make sure that it is managed by someone from the country concerned. The same will be true for our new operation in Finland.

Our new subsidiary will have a .... manager.

10 Although our company was originally Swedish, four years ago we transferred all of our operations to Switzerland and re-registered over there.

The company is no longer ....

2 Nations

Study the information contained in the following chart and then complete the passage below.

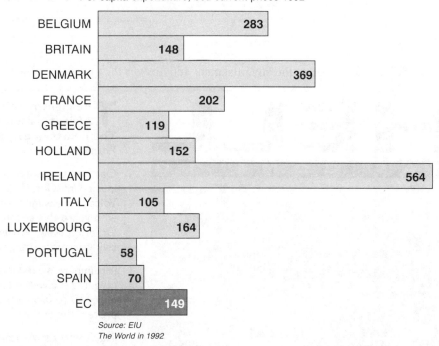

ALCOHOLIC BEVERAGES

Per capita expenditure, ecu current prices 1992

BELGIUM	283
BRITAIN	148
DENMARK	369
FRANCE	202
GREECE	119
HOLLAND	152
IRELAND	564
ITALY	105
LUXEMBOURG	164
PORTUGAL	58
SPAIN	70
EC	149

Source: EIU
The World in 1992

The chart above illustrates the different levels of per capita expenditure on alcoholic beverages for different EC member countries in 1992. As you can see, the lowest amount spent was by the [1]........................ with the [2]........................ in next position at 70 ecus. Amongst those nations who spent the most on this type of product were the [3]........................ who were almost two hundred ecus ahead of their nearest rivals, the [4]........................ . In comparison, the expenditure of the [5]........................ was only half that of the leading country. Both the [6]........................ and the [7]........................ were within five ecus of the EC national average of 149.

WRITING   Managers know that in order to run their organisations effectively, it is very important to discipline their schedules carefully. In a short composition, explain how you manage your time on a daily basis. In your composition, you should try to answer the following questions:

- How do you plan your daily schedule?
- Do you meet deadlines easily?
- Do you work towards long-term goals?
- Would you say you are an organised person?

- Are you in control most days and in most situations?
- In which situations do you have difficulty?

Advertising and Marketing

READING   Study the advertisement and answer the questions which follow.

HELL HAS COME TO PARADISE

African Wildlife Foundation,
1717 Massachusetts Avenue, N.W.,
Suite 602, Washington, DC20036.
Or Call (202) 265-8393 for
more information.

AFRICAN WILDLIFE FOUNDATION

The nightmare of anarchy and bloodshed in the African nation of Rwanda defies description. The hearts of everyone at the African Wildlife Foundation go out to the people of Rwanda.

Our hearts also go out to the mountain gorillas, popularized in the film 'Gorillas in the Mist', who live in the Parc Des Volcans in Rwanda. Understandably, many of the park rangers who guard this endangered species fled during the fighting. Others bravely remained at their post through most of the civil war, monitoring the gorillas' whereabouts and well-being.

It is imperative for the gorillas' safety that these wardens and rangers receive the food and basic equipment they need in order to return to the park and set up regular patrols to protect the gorillas.

That's why the African Wildlife Foundation has established the Mountain Gorilla Emergency Fund. Our goal is to raise $85,000 to re-equip the rangers, and provide park personnel with food and equipment and money to live on for the next six months.

Please send a donation to the Mountain Gorilla Emergency Fund c/o African Wildlife Foundation, 1717 Massachusetts Avenue, N.W., Suite 602, Washington, D.C. 20036, or call (202) 265-8393 for more information.

Together, we can ensure the survival of one of Earth's true wildlife wonders – the magnificent mountain gorillas of Rwanda!

1 Find words in the advertisement which match the definitions below:

a   a horrible, distressing condition or event ....

b   a person who works in a national park or forest (2 different words) ....

c   to run away from (past participle) ....

d   to check systematically ....

e   the approximate location of someone or something ....

f   urgent; obligatory ....

g   to guarantee ....

2 How has the civil war in Rwanda affected the well-being of the gorillas in Rwanda?

....

3 What is needed in order to protect the gorillas?

....

4 What does the advertisement request the reader to do?

....

5 The mountain gorilla of Rwanda is an endangered species, which means that it may no longer exist in a few years. Can you think of any other endangered species and why they are endangered?

....

6 This is a noncommercial advertisement run by the AWF. Look at the following list of objectives of advertising and tick (✓) the ones which are specific to noncommercial advertising as opposed to product advertising.

■ stimulate sales
■ communicate an idea or opinion
■ improve product image
■ inform public of a cause
■ remind people to buy again

■ stimulate requests for information
■ communicate product characteristics
■ improve public attitude
■ inform public of new product
■ remind people to give again

VOCABULARY

1 Advertising slogans

Read the slogans and match them with the products or institutions for which you think they were actually used. Note how you made your decision.

1 Get into our bed and sleep better ....

2 Down under: it's home to us ....

3 Would Mrs O'Brien trust her precious soles to just anyone? ....

4 I went to work and left my wrinkles at home ....

5 Waist disposal unit ....

6 M.P. *(Member of Parliament)* involved in cover up ....

7 Prices that won't leave you speechless ....

8 The architects of time ....

9 Could you be a more inspiring leader? ....

10 The focus of attention ....

a cosmetic cream

b the Army

c white correction fluid

d socks

e watches

f Australian airline company

g video camera (camcorder)

h mattress

i telephones

j 'Nordic ski' exerciser

17

2 Circle the word that does not belong in each horizontal group. You may need to reread the text on page 36 of the Students' Book.

1 promotion	export	pricing	packaging
2 clause	client	contract	brochure
3 slogan	fee	money	pay
4 star	executive	actor	celebrity
5 to endorse	to afford	to promote	to support
6 computer	television	commercial	advertisement
7 publicity	image	reputation	agent
8 to plummet	to fall	to rise	to drop

3 Match the words on the left with the words on the right to make compound nouns which are commonly used in advertising. You may need a dictionary to help you. After you have completed the exercise, give a brief definition of each compound noun.

1 market	5 status	**a** audience	**e** research
2 mass	6 sales	**b** time	**f** mail
3 target	7 prime	**c** media	**g** promotion
4 direct		**d** symbol	

LANGUAGE FOCUS

Gerund or infinitive?

Put the verbs in brackets in the passage in either the gerund or infinitive form.

Research conducted in 23 countries by an association called Europanel has shown that social and demographic factors as well as the marketing strategies of multinational food and drink companies tend ¹ _to make_ (make) the lifestyles and eating habits of different European countries alike.

There are several reasons for the increasing uniformity in consumption in Europe: birth rates keep on ² .... (fall) (Spain's birth rate is 9.8 per thousand, compared with 12.1 in 1984), thus creating smaller households which rely on ³ .... (use) microwaves and convenience foods. The number of one-person households in Europe also continues ⁴ .... (grow) rapidly (in Sweden, for example, 40% of homes are now one-person households, compared with 29% in 1984).

The aggressive marketing strategies of multinationals can also ⁵ .... (play) a key role in ⁶ .... (change) buying habits. After ⁷ .... (win) a major share of a market, companies often decide ⁸ .... (expand) into new markets and make every effort ⁹ .... (attract) new consumers. For instance, the French, who used ¹⁰ .... (have) croissants for breakfast, now enjoy ¹¹ .... (eat) breakfast cereals (sales of cereals keep on ¹² .... (grow) in France each year). The British have become fond of ¹³ .... (drink) mineral water and Spaniards are beginning ¹⁴ .... (buy) frozen pizzas and tomato ketchup more than ever.

With companies looking for new markets and increased choice for consumers, Europe's gastronomic diversity may ¹⁵ .... (end).

WRITING Read the following four excerpts from advertisements. As you read them, underline the words or phrases which make you believe that the claims they make are misleading or fraudulent. Then choose one and write a short letter to the Advertising Standards Authority in which you express your disapproval of such advertisements and say why you think newspapers should not run them.

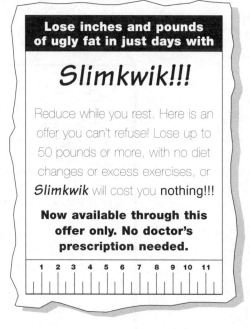

Thanks to the success of a discovery in the USA, many bald men are now enjoying the benefit once more of having a
full head of their own growing hair!

Before   **After**

These remarkable results are achievable through the daily application of a solution to the scalp.
Further details may be obtained by completing the coupon.

MALE EGYPTIAN MUMMY

*2,400 years old
with gilt cartonage mask
and
multi-coloured
sarcophagus. Appraisal:
'in exceptional
condition'.*

Send *$10*
for colour photos
and full description.

**Lose inches and pounds
of ugly fat in just days with**

Slimkwik!!!

Reduce while you rest. Here is an offer you can't refuse! Lose up to 50 pounds or more, with no diet changes or excess exercises, or *Slimkwik* will cost you **nothing!!!**

Now available through this offer only. No doctor's prescription needed.

*A **dream holiday** in magical*

☼ Spain! ☼

*Rent a traditional Spanish country house with pool in a remote mountain village, near beautiful beaches. To benefit from the unbelievably low prices which only our agency offers, fill in the form and **send it today.***

You won't find an opportunity like this one again!

Franchising

READING Read the information about Ben & Jerry's and answer the questions opposite.

Ben & Jerry's Statement of Mission

PRODUCT

To make, distribute & sell the finest quality all-natural ice cream & related products in a wide variety of innovative flavours made from Vermont dairy products.

ECONOMIC

To operate the Company on a sound financial basis of profitable growth, increasing value for our shareholders & creating career opportunities & financial rewards for our employees.

SOCIAL

To operate the Company in a way that actively recognises the central role that business plays in the structure of society by initiating innovative ways to improve the quality of life of a broad community: local, national & international.

 Ben & Jerry's is a company based in Vermont, USA, which makes all-natural ice cream and frozen yogurt. It was founded in 1978 by two childhood friends, Ben Hogen & Jerry Greenfield, who started with a $12,000 investment, $4,000 of which was borrowed. They soon became popular for their unique flavours such as Chunky Monkey and Cherry Garcia. The company is a success today and remains determined to follow its 'Statement of Mission'.

The company distributes its products in all 50 states and also has nearly 100 independent franchise scoop shops in the USA and Canada, whose annual sales exceed $26 million. The franchisees buy a ten-year licence to use the company name and graphics. Common marketing strategies are used by all franchises and employees are trained in the same skills and attitudes. Although franchises account for only 5% of sales, they play an important role in informing the company which products are selling and giving detailed customer feedback. A few years ago, the company decided that the franchising option, which went through some periods of rapid growth (40 new stores in one year alone), would not be pursued for a while so that the business support services needed by existing store owners could be offered. Today, new franchise outlets are opening but at a slower pace.

Most of Ben & Jerry's franchisees are experienced, committed operators whose stores are their primary source of income. The average scoop shop has sales of $300,000. They are not only vital business partners, but also play an important role since they project a direct, caring image of the company to customers. The shops, whose customers value their presence in their community, actively participate in many local events and campaigns (aid to homeless shelters, childcare facilities, etc.). As one franchisee put it, 'Working for Ben & Jerry's is working with a company with a tremendous heart.'

1 Where do the ingredients used in Ben & Jerry's products come from?

....

2 How are employees affected by the company Statement of Mission?

....

3 How does Ben & Jerry's see its role in the structure of society?

....

4 How do the franchises play a role in product development?

....

5 Why did the company stop opening franchise shops a few years ago?

....

6 How do franchises participate in the company's social mission?

....

VOCABULARY Complete the crossword. The answers can be found in the text on page 45 of the Students' Book and in the vocabulary exercise on page 46.

Clues

Across

3 The main part of a land mass as opposed to an island
7 The opposite of 'pessimistic'
10 Abbreviation of 'Master of Arts'
12 A document giving permission to make or sell something
14 A shop that sells products made by a particular company
16 A shop (American English)
18 Not limited to one country
19 Indefinite article
20 To be in charge of a company
22 Abbreviation of United Press International
23 A way of doing something
26 Successful, prosperous

Down

1 Specific to one place
2 A spectacular increase in business
3 Past simple of 'to meet'
5 Abbreviation of American Telephone and Telegraph
6 A period of ten years
8 A person associated with another, often in business
9 The opposite of 'out'
11 The opposite of 'western'
13 To reduce
15 To give something to someone temporarily, on the condition that it will be returned
17 Ready to do something
18 Informal
20 A competitor
21 Definite article
24 The opposite of 'up'
25 'Either we spend more money on advertising ....we will lose business.'

LANGUAGE
FOCUS

Relative pronouns

Complete the following short description of the American franchise 'Imagine That!!!' with the appropriate relative pronouns. You should also indicate (–) in which cases it is possible to omit the relative pronoun.

Imagine That!!! is a new American franchise [1] _____whose_____ customers all have one thing in common: they are all aged between 2 and 10!

"Where learning comes into play!"

The idea for the company, [2] _____ was started in April 1993, was the brainchild of two married couples, the Bodnars and the

Piersons, [3] _____ all thought that there was room on the market for a new concept in children's entertainment.

As Mrs Pierson says: 'We wanted to start a fun business [4] _____ our kids would enjoy and could get involved with. We wanted to have someplace

fun, where parents could bring their children and [5] _____ would also be educational.'

At present the company's first 'Discovery Center' is located in East Hanover, New Jersey but there are already plans to open a second, franchised operation in the near future. The centers themselves,

[6] _____ occupy 14,000 square feet, contain 38 exhibits

[7] _____ children can interact with.

In the 'Kidport,' children can sit in the cockpit of a real Piper airplane and handle the controls. At the 'Corner Grocery' they can do their own shopping [8] _____ they can even pay for with pretend money.

Imagine That!!! also aims to familiarise children with some of the

difficulties [9] _____ face handicapped people in their daily lives. The 'Disabled' exhibit gives them the chance to handle Braille books and to attend handicap awareness demonstrations.

The company is expanding actively and is keen to hear from people

[10] _____ would be interested in taking out an Imagine That!!! franchise. Although the cost of opening an Imagine That!!! unit will vary according to size and location, future franchisees should be prepared to make a total investment of between $385,000 and $425,000.

WRITING You are interested in finding out more about 'Imagine That!!!' because you think that the concept would work well in your own country.

Prepare a list of the additional information that you need about the franchisor and of any specific questions that you would like to ask. It may be useful to refer to the activity on page 51 of the Students' Book.

Now, using your list, write a short letter to Imagine That!!! in which you present yourself as a potential franchisor or master franchisor and then request information on the various points. Refer to page 145 of the Students' Book for help with the layout of your letter.

Address:

Imagine That!!!

200 Rt 10W

East Hanover

New Jersey

USA

Japan and the Business World

READING Read the text on the right and answer the questions below.

1 Which verb in the first paragraph could replace the verb 'to slip' in the title of the article? ....

2 Find the words in the text which correspond to the following definitions:

■ to cut; to reduce *(para. 4)*

....

■ a sudden decline *(para. 4)*

....

■ capable of facing difficult situations; strong *(para. 4)* ....

3 How many times has the average workweek in Japan slipped below 40 hours in the past 20 years?

....

....

4 How do we know that the average workweek has declined?

....

....

5 What two reasons are given for the decrease in the hours worked per week in Japan?

....

....

Japan's Workweek Slips Below 40 Hours

Bloomberg Business News

1 TOKYO – The Labour Ministry said Wednesday that the average number of hours worked weekly by Japanese employees fell below 40 last year for the first time since its survey began nearly two decades ago.

2 The average work week in 1993 was down 12 minutes from 1992, at 39 hours and 51 minutes. The figures were based on a survey of 5,300 businesses.

3 When the ministry began the survey in 1975, the average time worked each week was 42 hours and eight minutes. Ten years later, the workweek was down to 41 hours and 45 minutes, and it has fallen steadily since.

4 The shorter workweek partly reflects government efforts to emphasize leisure time and improve the Japanese quality of life. But while government attempts to trim the workweek have had some effect, economists said Japan's longest economic slump since the end of World War II was a major factor.

5 The so-called lifetime employment system characteristic of Japanese labor practices has prevented many companies from making major cuts in their work forces. As a result, companies have had to try to reduce costs by cutting down the hours worked by each employee.

6 The average workweek in the financial, insurance and real-estate sectors was among the lowest of all fields included in the survey. These are the same sectors that have suffered the most from the recession.

7 Meanwhile, employees in fields that have proven more resilient to the recession have experienced less of a drop in hours on the job.

8 The Labour Ministry also said Japanese workers' average number of days off rose to 19.9 in 1993 and 19.5 a year earlier. Still, old habits die hard: Last year, paid vacation days rose to an average of 16.3, the ministry said; but only 9.1, or 56 percent, of those days marked for vacation were actually taken. *International Herald Tribune*

6 Which sectors have the shortest working hours and why?

....

7 What is ironic about the rise in the number of paid vacation days in Japan?

....

VOCABULARY   Study the following examples taken from the text on page 54 of the Students' Book:

That's the Japanese word for death from **overwork**. (lines 6-7)

Hardly a week goes by without a grim report about some **overzealous** *worker in the prime of his life who could not just say no to* **overtime**. (lines 21-25)

In some cases, *over* used as the first element of a word means an excess of what is normal (as in the examples above).

Complete the sentences, using the nouns, verbs and adverbs from the list to replace the words or phrases in brackets. You may have to change the form of certain words.

overall	overdue	overnight
overbook	overestimate	overseas
overcharge	overhaul	overtime
overdraft	overheads	overview

1 We arrived at the hotel at 6:00 p.m. and stayed .... *(until the following morning)*.

2 Last week everybody in the department had to work .... *(extra hours)*.

3 The speaker began by giving us an .... *(general presentation)* of the situation.

4 .... *(in general)* we have been disappointed with the results.

5 The company is planning to send three of its senior UK managers to work .... *(abroad)*.

6 The payment we were expecting is .... *(late)*.

7 Our bank has agreed to let us have an .... *(debit)* of £15,000 on our account.

8 The .... *(costs of running the business)* are likely to increase next year.

9 The .... *(review and modification)* of our order processing system has saved us a lot of time and money.

10 We .... *(judged too greatly)* the cost of the new electronic mail system: actually, it was much cheaper than we had expected.

11 The airline .... *(took too many reservations)*: we therefore had to wait for the next flight to Rome.

12 Our supplier tends to .... *(ask for too high prices)*: the invoice for the office furniture should have been for £9,500 instead of £11,100.

LANGUAGE FOCUS

Expressing contrast

Correct the following sentences. There may be more than one possible answer for each sentence.

1 In spite of the American car sales have overtaken the Japanese for the first time since 1979, Japan dominates the fast growing East Asian market.

Even though American car sales have overtaken the Japanese for the first time since 1979, Japan dominates the fast growing East Asian market.

2 Although their hostility towards Japan, some governments readily accept Japanese investment.

3 In spite of the Japanese may say 'yes' at a meeting, it does not mean that they agree with you, but that they want you to continue.

4 Despite foreign speakers are advised to show respect for their Japanese audience, many of them begin their speeches with a joke.

5 The American manager was dressed too informally at the seminar, despite he knew that the Japanese wear conservative suits while making speeches.

6 Many Japanese business executives say that they believe strongly in free trade, though Japan's continuing preference for buying at home.

7 Even though the fact that gift giving is a common practice in Japan, the gifts should never be opened in front the giver.

8 In spite of the negotiations lasted a very long time, the project for a merger between the Japanese and German commercial banks failed.

9 Despite he has a degree from Tokyo's prestigious Gakushuin University, he fears that the recession will make it difficult to find a job.

10 Imports have been rising in Japan although the recession.

....

....

WRITING   **Memo writing**

The following memo does not respect the basic rules of memo writing. First identify five mistakes in the memo. Then decide how the memo can be improved in line with the guidelines on page 58 of the Students' Book and rewrite it.

MEMORANDUM

RICHARDSON Automotives

39 Bainbridge Road, London SE8 9KH
Telephone: 0171-548-1000

To: All members of staff

From: John Palmer, Managing Director

Subject: Telephone calls

The company has been loosing thousands of pounds each month on phone calls, and unless everyone makes an effort to use the telephone correctly, we will have to adapt new measures to limit personal calls.

I have carefully examined last month's telephone bill and I am quiet alarmed by what I have found. The figures show that as far as the destination of calls is concerned, 10% are to our Milan subsidiary, 15% are local calls and 75% are long distance national calls outside our dealer network. This means that 75% of the calls are personal calls, and these calls tend to be the longest and the most expensive for the company.

Its each staff member's responsibility to use the phone for business purposes only and to realise that the abuse I have just mentioned costs the company thousands of pounds each month. I am counting on your co-operation.

JP

Business and the Environment

READING

1 The sentences below are extracts from a text about B & Q, a British Do-It-Yourself store. Read them and replace the words in brackets with an appropriate word from the following list.

activities	manufacture	disposal	profits	impact	project
initiatives	retailer	issues	strategy	levels	suppliers

a Indeed its numerous awards for environmental ¹ .... *(innovative actions)* show how seriously it has considered these complex ² .... *(controversial questions)*.

b This unique British ³ .... *(a company selling goods to the general public)* specialises in selling home repair products.

c B & Q therefore chose to adapt its business ⁴ .... *(a plan of action)* and to pay closer attention to environmental ⁵ .... *(the effect of one thing on another)*.

d This means that all ⁶ .... *(companies selling products to other companies)* must know what damage results from their ⁷ .... *(different actions)* and must plan to reduce that impact.

e This may occur at different ⁸ .... *(moments or stages)*; the acquisition of the raw materials, the ⁹ .... *(production)* of a product, its use and its ¹⁰ .... *(elimination)*.

f One example of such an operation is in Papua New Guinea where a ¹¹ .... *(a plan that is being carried out)* with the Bainings people has shown that it is possible for them to manage their own resources economically and to generate ¹² .... *(money made by a business venture)* which can be reinvested in the community itself.

2 Now insert these six extracts in the appropriate positions in the text on the opposite page. In the spaces provided, write in the letters (**a - f**) that correspond to each extract.

1 (............) Since many of the items that it offers for sale are made from natural materials such as wood, the company has since 1991 adopted an environmental policy in order to reduce the damage that may result from its various activities. **2** (............) In many cases the products may well have had an effect on some of the key areas of environmental concern such as deforestation and global warming.

3 (............) In 1991 it became apparent that almost 90% of the companies supplying timber-based products to B & Q were not prepared to reveal their sources. The company therefore set itself the target that by the end of 1995 all of its timber would come from well-managed forests across the world. **4** (............) Failure to do so leads to delisting.

B & Q has also assisted local communities in some countries to set up their own small scale companies to manage their forest resources. **5** (............)

The company would be the first to admit that it is almost impossible for any business to be completely green. Nevertheless B & Q is proud of what has already been achieved both abroad and at home (25% of its total waste is recycled). **6** (............) There is, however, still a long way to go, or as they put it themselves, 'The more environmental problems we solve, the more we find worth solving.'

VOCABULARY   Derivation

Look at the following words taken from the text on page 63 of the Students' Book and complete the table. You may need a dictionary to help you. Then complete sentences 1-6 using words from the table.

VERB	NOUN	ADJECTIVE
___	environmentalist environment environmentalism	environmental
....	protester	___
....	founder	___
to contribute	....	___
to mobilise	....	....
to educate	....	....
___	....	political
....	....	developing
....	supplier	___
___	....	unemployed
to measure	....	....

1 Many companies do research to .... ways of reducing air and water pollution.

2 Next weekend an environmental group is organising a(n) .... against dumping of waste into rivers.

3 This conservation group has a(n) .... programme which teaches children about endangered species.

4 Every year, we make a(n) .... to a well-known wildlife association.

5 The German 'Die Grünen' party has a strong influence in green .... everywhere.

6 Most major cities .... the quality of the air every day.

LANGUAGE FOCUS

The passive

Complete the following passage using the appropriate passive forms of the verbs in the table below.

Paragraph 1	encourage	launch	collect	transport		
Paragraph 2	represent	analyse	compose			
Paragraph 3	throw away	design	recycle	reduce	make	transform
Paragraph 4	send	buy	take	install		
Paragraph 5	prove	purchase	make	adopt	achieve	

In 1993 a campaign [1] _was launched_ by the UK government to reduce the amount of domestic waste. Households [2] _____ to recycle certain waste products and to sort and prepare others for collection at specific sites. From there they will then [3] _____ and [4] _____ to industrial waste treatment plants for recycling.

In Britain today, when the contents of the average domestic dustbin [5] _____ , we find that, in terms of weight, 35% of the total [6] _____ of paper and cardboard, 22% of kitchen waste, 12% of plastics 10% of glass 10% of dust and ashes. 9% [7] _____ by metals and the remaining 2% by textiles.

There are only a few items of domestic waste that can't [8] _____ . One common example is disposable nappies which, as their name suggests, have [9] _____ to [10] _____ . However, a lot of progress could [11] _____ especially towards reducing the quantities of kitchen waste which can easily [12] _____ into a useful compost for use as a garden fertiliser. Indeed, if more people chose to do this then the weight of the average dustbin would [13] _____ quite significantly.

In glass products the situation is more encouraging as nearly 20% of the glass that [14] _____ every year in the country [15] _____ for recycling. This is partly due to the presence of more than 12,000 bottle banks which [16] _____ since 1977. However, the same is not true for tin and aluminium cans where, according to recent figures, only 10% to 16% of used containers [17] _____ for recycling.

It is clear that the quantities of waste will only decrease if efforts [18] _____ both by households and also by local government authorities. Special equipment such as collection trucks must [19] _____ . Such systems have already [20] _____ with considerable success in the last few years in several regions of Europe and their value [21] _____ . However, the question remains: will the UK government's target of a 25% reduction [22] _____ in the near future? Only time will tell!

WRITING   You have read an article concerning two studies which found that 10,000 porpoises are killed each year in the seas around Britain. Boats from Britain, Ireland and Denmark use a technique which consists in leaving nets up to six miles long on the sea bed for several hours. Porpoises tend to feed on the sea bed which is why they get caught in the nets and drown. Fishing, rather than pollution, appears to be the biggest threat to these highly intelligent marine mammals.

Write a letter to The Ministry of Agriculture, Fisheries and Food (MAFF) in which you first express your feelings or opinions on the subject. You should then develop the arguments suggested below in the body of your letter.

■ There is a need for research carried out by universities and marine mammal organisations to make nets more 'porpoise friendly', for example by restricting the length of nets.

■ Action should be taken by MAFF and other government departments and agencies responsible for fisheries and the marine environment, i.e. steps to control and limit the size of catches. You realise, however, that the demand for fish is high and that fishermen need to make a living.

■ The actions to conserve whales and dolphins should also be taken into account for porpoises to maintain the natural balance of the seas.

Remember that you do not want to offend the fishermen who allowed observers on their boats. This could make future studies difficult.

Add as many other ideas as you wish, perhaps based on articles you have read or television programmes that you have seen on related subjects. Pay close attention to grammar, spelling and punctuation. Do not forget the date.

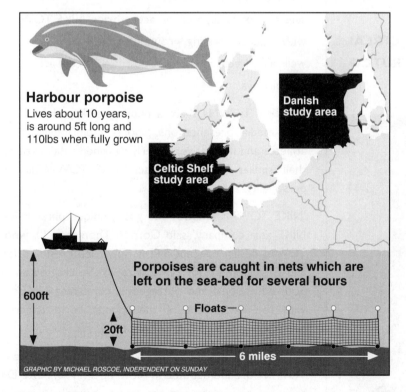

MAFF Address:

Whitehall Place

London SW2

Your Address:

8 Mulberry Crescent

Hayes

Middlesex UB4 OQA

Retailing

READING   **1** The following text is part of a press release about Nike town, an original retailing concept created by the American sportswear company Nike, Inc. Complete the text using the words which you will find in scrambled form in the margin. All these words can be found in the text on page 71 of the Students' Book.

ORTSE

RBDNA

IDRAETN

NILE

ETRLAI

SMERUTCO

NIKE TOWN: A RETROSPECTIVE

At the core of a NIKE TOWN ¹ ....*store*........ is a simple objective: enhance the NIKE ² .... image. NIKE TOWN sales associates are friendly and fully ³ .... to know everything about every product NIKE makes, which is crucial since NIKE TOWN is home to NIKE's entire ⁴ .... of footwear and an extensive selection of its apparel and accessories. NIKE TOWNs also provide NIKE with valuable testing ground for new ⁵ .... ideas, as well as direct ⁶ .... feedback on products, services and displays.

All NIKE TOWNs share a number of key physical elements - high-tech multi-media presentations, sports memorabilia from the world's top athletes and innovative, cleverly designed retail fixtures. However, despite their similar foundations, each NIKE TOWN has an entirely different personality.

'NIKE TOWNs embody the goals, unique personality and philosophy of NIKE as a company,' said Gordon Thompson III, who created the NIKE TOWN design concept and is now Vice President for Research, Design and Development for NIKE, Inc. 'We've created an environment that is both educational and outrageous, combining NIKE's product innovation with the excitement of the sports world to create an interactive, entertaining shopping experience.'

As additional NIKE TOWNS have opened across the country since NIKE TOWN Portland debuted in November 1990, NIKE Design has continued to inject new ideas and the latest technology into these 'sports retail theatres.' Therefore, in order to look ahead to the future of NIKE TOWNs, it's important to look back to see how the concept has evolved.

NIKE TOWN Chicago

CSSSEUC

Flushed with the 7................................ of its first NIKE TOWN in Portland, NIKE Retail quickly set its sights on Chicago with a prime location on the city's celebrated 'Magnificent Mile.' Located at 669 North Michigan Avenue, NIKE TOWN Chicago blew into the Windy City on July 2, 1992, and in a matter of months was named Chicago's top retail tourist attraction by Crain's Chicago Business.

ERAUQS

At 68,000 8................................ feet spread over five floors, NIKE TOWN Chicago is more than three times the size of its

DIOVE

Portland predecessor and includes a 9................................ theatre and a basketball half-court, perfect for 'test-driving' a new pair of shoes. While the

TKCOS

top two floors are primarily for 10................................, customer

IESREVC

11................................ and administration, the first three floors are a dazzling array of 18 individual pavilions, nearly all in sight of each other thanks to the three-story atrium that rises from Town Square.

NIKE TOWN's Future

REPOETA

By the end of this decade, NIKE Retail plans to 12................................ from 10 to 15 NIKE TOWNs in major sports markets across the United States (NIKE policy forbids releasing the names of the cities currently under scrutiny until a lease agreement has been signed). As for international growth, NIKE is considering the possibility but no target dates or locations have been announced.

NPOSE

By the time the last of the NIKE TOWNs 13................................ in the United States a few years from now, it might look radically different from its 'ancestor' in Portland. With the advent of virtual reality, interactive shopping and other technological advances to come, the only sure thing is that future NIKE TOWNs will continue to ride the cutting edge of retail design and innovation.

2 Decide if the following statements are true (T) or false (F), or if the statement gives information that is not provided in the text (N).

1 Nike Towns provide an opportunity to try out new selling techniques. ....

2 All Nike towns have the same personality. ....

3 The first Nike Town opened in Chicago. ....

4 Reebok, Nike's rival, is also going to open similar stores. ....

5 Nike Towns try to make shopping an exciting experience. ....

6 Nike towns cost a lot of money to create and to maintain. ....

7 Many people visit the Nike Towns. ....

8 Nike is considering expanding by the year 2000. ....

9 A Nike Town will be opened in London in 1996. ....

VOCABULARY

The following sentences are taken from the text on page 71 of the Students' Book. Match the words in bold with their opposite meanings in the right-hand column.

*The answer is Richer Sounds, a ¹ **little-known**, privately owned, cut-price retailer of hi-fi equipment. (lines 4-6)*

*The man behind Richer Sounds' ² **success** is founder, managing director and 98% shareholder Julian Richer. (lines 23-25)*

*I bought a ³ **second-hand** Bang & Olufsen for £10. (lines 40-41)*

*Richer Sounds sells ⁴ **discounted** hi-fi from ⁵ **tiny**, ⁶ **basic** shops with low overheads. (lines 47-48)*

*It buys either end-of-line ranges which manufacturers are hoping to ⁷ **off-load** before the next, cosmetically different, model arrives from Japan, or small orders of ⁸ **current** models which, perhaps because of poor stock management, the manufacturer is prepared to sell at a reduced price. (lines 63-70)*

*⁹ **First-time** hi-fi buyers get a call to check that they have plugged in the equipment correctly. (lines 109-111)*

.... **a** full-priced

.... **b** huge

.... **c** repeat

.... **d** new

.... **e** keep

.... **f** failure

.... **g** old

.... **h** famous

.... **i** sophisticated

LANGUAGE FOCUS

1 Make or Do?

Complete the following sentences with the correct form of *make* or *do*. You may need a dictionary to help you.

1 Store managers ....*make*............ decisions about which products to keep and which ones ....*to do*............ away with.

2 We .... arrangements with a store designer .... up our window displays.

3 Last year we .... well, despite the recession.

4 We .... a mistake by assuming that our products would sell well abroad.

5 I'm in charge of inventory and stock management. Who .... that job in your store?

6 We have met many suppliers, but we .... up our minds yet about which ones to work with.

7 We promise .... our best to have that item for you by the end of the week.

8 Although that company has almost the same name as ours, we have nothing .... with them.

9 You should .... certain that the customers are always satisfied.

10 In many cases, it .... sense to stock original products that cannot be found easily in other shops.

11 He .... a living as store manager for over 30 years and does not plan to retire yet.

12 Could you .... me a favour and work the morning shift?

13 .... workers redundant is never an easy task for a manager. ·

2 Adjectives + prepositions

Look at the sample taken from the Nike text, line 45: ... *it might look different* **from** *its 'ancestor' in Portland.* Many adjectives in English take certain prepositions when followed by nouns. Fill in the blanks below with the correct prepositions. You may need a dictionary to help you.

1 Although Leila is young, she is already successful ....*in*......... business.

2 It is necessary .... us to improve our after-sales service.

3 Is your computer compatible .... mine?

4 The customers are very critical .... some of the products we sell.

5 We must be attentive .... the needs of our customers.

6 We're certain .... the positive results that a national advertising campaign can have.

7 I was not aware .... the fact that these models no longer exist.

8 We are very satisfied .... this quarter's profits.

9 I'm interested .... a career in retailing.

10 We're quite concerned .... the problem of stock management.

11 Our customers are fond .... the 'personal touch' that we try to emphasise in each of our shops.

12 The neighbourhood residents seem enthusiastic .... the opening of the new shop.

WRITING

Write a short profile of a retail outlet where you like to shop and explain what makes it different from other shops which sell similar products.

Banking

READING   Read the advertisement for First Direct, the UK telephone bank, and then indicate which of the statements that follow accurately reflect the information contained in it (✓) and which do not (✗).

the more you stroke your cat, the more affectionate it becomes.

Cats are not affectionate by instinct, and need constant handling to break down their suspicion. Stroking works well; it soothes your cat by imitating the grooming action of a mother cat licking her kittens. Note: cats who are not stroked when young will be very resistant to stroking when they become adults.

first direct

as a first direct customer, you're always treated with courtesy.

If you're a traditional bank, you see the world in terms of branches. How is branch x doing, how is branch y performing, what can we do to help branch z? But First Direct is a telephone bank that doesn't have any branches, which means that we're able to look at the world in terms of our customers. Certainly, when we launched in 1989, we launched with the specific aim of

a customer focus

providing modern customers with their first appropriate banking service. One that's courteous: all our Banking Representatives are trained extensively to be polite, calm and friendly, One that's thoughtful: we're open 24 hours a day. 365 days a

24 hours a day

year so that you can bank whenever you remember, feel like it or need to. One that's fast: every Banking Representative has the authority to give you on-the-spot decisions and advice. One that's lean: because we have no expensive branches to maintain, we don't need to pass transaction charges on to our customers. One that's convenient: you can withdraw up to £500

free banking

per day from 7000 cash machines up and down the country, and you can pay your cheques in at any Midland branch or post them to us directly. And one that's innovative: for example, our automatic bill payment, where on receipt of a bill, you can

bill payment service

simply call us, tell us who to pay and how much to pay and leave the rest to us. Why such emphasis on the customer? Because we believe it's a genuine point of difference, and also a good way to grow our business – currently 89% of our customers recommend us to their friends. To find out more about the banking service that fits around your life, call the freephone number.

call us now

☎ **0800 24 24 24**

1 If you wish to deposit a cheque in your account you can send it to First Direct through the post. ....

2 First Direct was created to provide an alternative to traditional banking. ....

3 First Direct has no arrangements for its customers to use the facilities of other banks.

....

4 Banking Representatives are only entitled to carry out transactions on behalf of the bank's customers. ....

5 First Direct customers may take out more than £4,000 in cash per week. ....

6 The operating costs of First Direct are lower than for traditional banks. ....

7 First Direct never closes. ....

8 The majority of First Direct customers are satisfied with the bank and its services.

....

VOCABULARY   Match a word from each of the columns below to form expressions that could be used to replace the words in italics in sentences A-I. Write the answers in the space provided after each sentence (there are two answers to F).

VERBS				NOUNS			
1	check	6	raise	a	capital	f	the bill
2	provide	7	change	b	cash	g	interest
3	move	8	withdraw	c	foreign money	h	a statement
4	pay	9	earn	d	funds	i	shares
5	order	10	issue	e	a loan	j	balances

A With the new computer system, customers can *consult their accounts* to see how much money they have available. ....*1 j*..........

B Next week we will have to *settle the invoice* for the supplies that we received last month.

....

C I would like to *arrange to have a copy of all the transactions on my account* for the month of August this year. ....

D With the new card you can *take out up to £100 pounds* whenever you need it.

....

E The advantage of this account is that you will *receive a percentage* on the money that you deposit. ....

F In order to *increase financial resources* the company intends to *sell units of its capital* on the stock market. ....

G Nowadays it is possible to *transfer money* between different accounts using an electronic banking system installed in your home. ....

H My bank has agreed to *give me the money I need*, repayable over three years, to help me get the business started. ....

I It doesn't matter if the banks are closed when I arrive because I'm sure that at the hotel in Zurich I'll be able to *convert some dollars* into Swiss Francs. ....

LANGUAGE FOCUS

First and second conditional

Read each statement and use the information to complete the sentence that follows it by putting the verbs in brackets into the appropriate conditional form.

1 You have a £500 overdraft and have just received a letter from the bank asking you to reduce this by £200 by the end of the month. Otherwise they will start legal proceedings against you.

If you *do not reduce* (not reduce) your overdraft, the bank .... *will start* ....(start) legal proceedings.

2 One of your clients has written to you applying for a personal loan. However, she has not included enough information about her financial situation for you to decide whether or not to approve the loan.

If you .... (have) more complete information, you ....
(be able to) make a decision.

3 You have just received a selection of press articles about your bank. Two of them are in German. Unfortunately Jack Wubben, who is the only person in the office who speaks German, is on holiday.

If Jack Wubben .... (be) here, he................................... (translate) the articles.

4 For the second year running, the results of your bank have been very disappointing.

If the situation .... (not improve) significantly next year, the bank

.... (have to) consider closing some of its branches.

5 One of your major business clients has just hinted that it is prepared to change banks unless you arrange more favourable credit terms.

If you .... (not provide) them with cheaper credit, you ....
(lose) one of your best customers.

6 A bank representative has just refused your request for a £2,000 loan because you do not have enough money in your savings account.

If you .... (had) more money on deposit, the bank .... (lend) you the £2,000.

7 Your bank manager has just told you that she can only lend you £5,000 to enable you to buy a new car. The car you want costs £11,000 and you only have £4,000 of your own money available.

If you .... (not find) the remaining £2,000 you .... (not be able to) buy it.

8 You have recently applied for a transfer from your present job in London to another position with the company's Scottish subsidiary.

If your application .... (be) successful, you .... (have to) move house to Edinburgh.

9   You are making arrangements with your bank for a holiday in Italy next month.

If you .... *(take)* traveller's cheques this .... *(cost)* less than if

you .... *(buy)* foreign currency.

10   A friend has invited you to join her as a partner in a new business venture. You feel that you do not have the necessary experience.

If you .... *(have)* more experience, you............................... *(accept)* her offer.

11   You are talking to a customer who has asked you to replace a lost credit card for the fifth time this year.

'If you .... *(lose)* your card again in the future, I'm afraid that the bank

.... *(refuse)* to issue a replacement.'

12   You are preparing your bank's monthly newsletter. You realise that you will not have enough space for a profile of a new board member.

If you .... *(have)* more space available, you .... *(include)* it in the newsletter.

WRITING

Your employer has informed you that you have been promoted and will be assigned to the head office in London at the end of the month. You have found a flat but will need to pay a three month deposit of £2,000. In addition to this, you will have to pay for the move and other expenses. Your new job will mean a salary rise of about 25%.

Write a letter to your bank manager explaining your situation and requesting authorisation for an overdraft. The current balance of your account is in credit. You should also request information about the procedures involved in transferring your account to a branch in Covent Garden in London.

Address:

The Manager

Greenwich Bank

45 High Street

Doncaster

DO4 6YJ

The Stock Exchange

READING

1 In each of the headlines that follow there are three missing words. Fill in the two gaps in each headline with a word from the list below. Use the definitions provided to help you.

loss	forecast (vb)	foreign	revenue
chairman	reach (vb)	aid (vb)	price
level (n)	purchase (n)	advances (vb)	pushes up

A _foreign_ **units** _aid_ [ ]
(from a different country) *(to give assistance, to help)*

B _revenue_ **Rise** _pushes up_ _advances_ [ ] **Profit**
(money received or earned) *(increases)*

C [ ] _loss_ **cuts 10% from**
(the opposite of profit)

stock _____
(the cost of something)

D [ ] **Shares** _reach_ **Record** _level_
(attain, get to) *(position)*

E [ ] _advances_ **on rumour of stock** _purchase_
(moves forward) *(the act of buying)*

F [ ] _chairman_ **warns of lower than**
(the head of a company)

forecast **profits**
(estimated in the future, projected)

2 Now read the newpaper articles which correspond to the headlines and complete each headline with the name of the company concerned.

General Electric Co. said Tuesday that third quarter profit jumped 13 percent as revenue increased in many of its core businesses.
GE said revenue rose at 11 of its 12 businesses. Seven reported double-digit gains in operating profits - notably plastics, motors, appliances and information systems.
At GE Capital Services, the company's financial services arm, earnings for the quarter rose 7 percent to $526 million.

The stock price of Heineken NV climbed Friday as the company said its first half earnings were up more than 40 per cent, partly because of a gain from the sale of its holdings in a drinks distributor. Heineken shares closed at an unprecedented 244.5 guilders.

Shares in Apple Computer Inc. soared yesterday after speculation that Motorola Inc. might make a substantial equity investment or take over the company.
Motorola announced on Tuesday that it intended to enter the personal computer business with a product based on the Power PC chip developed by Apple, Motorola and International Business Machines Corp.
Most analysts gave the rumour little credence, but nevertheless, Apple shares surged by $4.125 or 12.2 percent, to close at $37.875.

United Biscuits (Holdings) PLC said Thursday its pretax profit rose 11 percent, to £80.1 million in the first half, boosted by rising earnings at its Keebler subsidiary in America and other overseas operations.

The turbulence in the French drinks industry continued yesterday with Rémy Cointreau, a leading wine and spirits producer, warning on profits.
Rémy, which has interests in wines and spirits including Cointreau liqueur, had originally been expected to make net profits of about FFr 313 m for the present financial year.
However, Mr André Hériard Dubreuil, Rémy chairman, told shareholders at yesterday's annual general meeting that final profits may fall short of those originally forecast because of the 'uncertain economic climate' and the falling dollar.

Big losses on cut-price sales of surplus aircraft sent Fokker NV spinning much deeper into thered than expected and Fokker shares plunged more than 10 per cent Wednesday.
Fokker, 51 percent owned by Daimler-Benz AG, said it was unable to make a forecast on results for next year but did not expect the aviation market to recover in the immediate future.

VOCABULARY Read the following authentic newspaper headlines and decide in each case whether they reflect a good (+), average (o) or poor (-) performance of the company's shares on the Stock Exchange. You may need a dictionary to help you.

1 Jarvis plans £27m buy as profits leap ....

2 The Limited recovers with a 10% increase ....

3 UPF trebles to £4.11m ....

4 Ugland returns to the black with £1.28m ....

5 Aswa ahead at Y4.6bn after six months ....

6 Earnings at Hamleys on course ....

7 Matsushita expects Y85bn profit boost ....

8 Welpac dives to £1.2m loss ....

9 Philips surges to £193m in third quarter ....

10 Jump in Rhône-Poulenc income ....

11 Bibby falls £10.7 into the red ....

12 Sumitono Metal Mining tumbles ....

LANGUAGE FOCUS

Third conditional

Disneyland Paris, formerly Euro Disney, the France-based theme park, has recently had problems in different areas (share prices, losses, costs, decline in visitors, etc.). Complete each of the following sentences relating to Disneyland Paris by putting the verbs in brackets into third conditional structures.

1 Disneyland Paris personnel executives _would have avoided_ *(avoid)* disputes with trade unions over dress codes if they _had paid_ *(pay)* closer attention to the sensitive issue of personal appearance in the workplace in France.

2 If the company .... *(lower)* the prices of hotels and restaurants earlier, perhaps this .... *(encourage)* more visitors.

3 Some analysts believe that if Disneyland Paris .... *(implement)* a new marketing strategy and changes in management at an earlier stage, the visitors

.... *(spend)* more money on food and souvenirs while in the park.

4 Some people say that if Europeans .... *(understand)* more about the concept of Disneyland before it opened in April 1992, attendance figures

.... *(increase)*.

5 According to a financial analyst, if Disneyland Paris bankers .... *(not assemble)* a refinancing package, the company

.... *(make)* a loss of 2.17 billion French francs up to the end of September 1994.

6 Disneyland Paris's chairman. Philippe Bourgignon, said that if there

.... *(not be)* so much negative publicity about the traumatic restructuring of the company, the number of visitors

.... *(not drop)*.

7 Disneyland Paris .... *(follow)* its initial development plans

if the recession .... *(not hit)* the real estate market so hard.

8 If the Bundesbank

.... *(not keep)* European interest rates so high in the early 1990s, Euro Disney's debt

.... *(not jump)* to more than 20 billion French francs.

WRITING   Write a short article on the best European stock of 1994 for the stock market pages of a newspaper. Base your article on the information below, and be sure to give it a headline.

COMPANY:	Nokia
COUNTRY:	Finland
SECTOR:	Engineering
YEARLY % CHANGE IN SHARES:	+141.5%
REASONS:	Expansion of mobile telephone market and excellent sales.
	Company spent 1994 consolidating its position as global supplier of telecommunication equipment, in particular mobile telephone systems.
1995 FORECAST:	Further 30% rise.
NEXT BEST PERFORMERS:	Gas Natural (Spanish utilities company: +34.1%) and Fiat (Italian car manufacturer: +29.5%).

Corporate Alliances and Acquisitions

READING

Read the following extracts from an interview with Thomas Malm, president of Volvo's European market area. Match his answers with the corresponding questions in the list below.

a *How have Volvo fared in Europe over the past year?* ....

b *What about individual models?* ....

c *The UK is a very strong market for Volvo. Can you achieve that level of penetration in other countries in Europe?* ....

d *Can you explain about your relationship with Mitsubishi?* ....

e *Your company has built upon a strong reputation for safety, yet all car manufacturers now heavily push this angle. Is Volvo still ahead of the game?* ....

f *The side air-bag is a great innovation for Volvo. When will we see it as a standard fitment and being offered in more models than the 850?* ....

g *What about Volvo's involvement with motor sport?* ....

h *Volvo has just produced its most powerful road car ever, the T-5R. What is the thinking behind this model?* ....

1 'We are collaborating on a specific project which will result in a car being built in a brand-new plant in the Netherlands. The two cars will be different, but will rely upon a number of common components. We should see the new models in 18 months to two years' time.'

2 'People have discovered that the 850 is a car which provides a great deal of driving pleasure, and we see clearly that there are drivers who are looking for better performance. So the concept of the 850 coupled with more power works very well. This allows Volvo to position itself as a company which today produces some very interesting cars, without getting away from our reputation for safety.'

3 'Every manufacturer has had a couple of tough years, but things are going well for us, with a 20% overall increase in sales and increased market shares in almost all countries.'

4 'The 850 has been our great success, with volumes up by 77% over last year.'

5 'It will gradually be phased in as we build up production capacity. We don't want to rush into it as it must be perceived by the customer as giving added value.'

6 'Yes, I believe so. It is very easy for a company to install an air-bag and claim its cars are as safe as any other. But the situation is not so simple. In-built safety is much more complex and there we still have a lead.'

7 'That's new for us, at least in the past decade. For the moment we are just competing in the British Touring Car Championship, and our main aim is to gain experience.'

8 'We have been very successful in the UK because we started many years ago with a very good importer which established a strong image and dealer network for Volvo. We were fortunate that in the UK we never experienced the ups and downs we had in some other markets, where the independent importers weren't quite so professional.'

VOCABULARY

1 Circle the word that does not belong in each horizontal group. You may need to reread pages 98 and 99 of the Students' Book to help you.

1 alliance	foothold	partnership	merger
2 talks	negotiations	operations	discussions
3 corporation	company	network	firm
4 components	profits	money	capital
5 to plunge	to plummet	to fall	to increase
6 research	deal	agreement	understanding
7 to acquire	to withstand	to purchase	to buy

2 Choosing from the seven words which you circled in the previous exercise, complete the following sentences taken from the business press.

1 Pilkington, the UK-based glass maker, was one of the first western countries to gain a

.... in China after the 'open door policy' in 1979.

2 Hyundai Electronics America, a US subsidiary of the Hyundai group of South Korea,

has agreed to acquire the semiconductor .... of AT&T Global Information Solutions, for more than $300m.

3 Amstrad, the loss-making consumer electronics group, unable to .... fierce competition, is to stop selling its computers and fax machines in high street shops.

4 Volvo, the Swedish car and commercial vehicle maker, has announced that Asia was Volvo's 'number one priority' for geographic expansion. It had carried out .... with China National Heavy Truck and Shandong Automotive for joint ventures for the production of both trucks and .... in Shandong province. Volvo was now waiting for official approval for the project from Beijing.

5 Lufthansa, the German national airline, and Thai Airways International, created the largest international .... of air services yesterday when they signed a strategic alliance. Lufthansa's weekly passenger flights to Thailand will .... to 20 in a year's time from 15 now.

LANGUAGE FOCUS

Reported Speech

The following sentences are extracts from a speech given by Charles Lewis, the Marketing Manager of United Tobacco, at a meeting with members of his department. Put each one into reported speech.

1 'Let me refresh your memories about the importance of the Chinese market.' *(remind)*

   He reminded us that the Chinese market was important.

2 'I believe that China can be the world's most lucrative market.' *(claim)*

   ....

3 'That is why we established manufacturing joint ventures there as soon as possible, despite the difficulties involved.' *(explain)*

   ....

4 'Another point about the Chinese market is that the industry is dominated by China's state tobacco monopoly.' *(add)*

   ....

5 'I must now break some news: China is planning to ban cigarette advertising in the media and in public places.' *(announce)*

   ....

6 'I must draw your attention to the fact that the provisions of the new law will be more restrictive than those in many western countries.' *(point out)*

   ....

7 'I would say that the reason for the ban is that China wants to respect international standards more.' *(think)*

   ....

8 'I really must make it very clear that this ban can certainly make it harder for the company to attract smokers away from the Chinese brand.' *(stress)*

   ....

9 'I guarantee that the department has already looked into other alternatives to advertising.' *(promise)*

   ....

10 'I have to make you aware of the danger of this law.' *(warn)*

   ....

WRITING You work in the Media Planning Department of United Tobacco and have been asked to write a short article for the company's 'in-house' newsletter. Use the sentences you wrote in the previous exercise, along with some of the notes below which you took during the meeting.

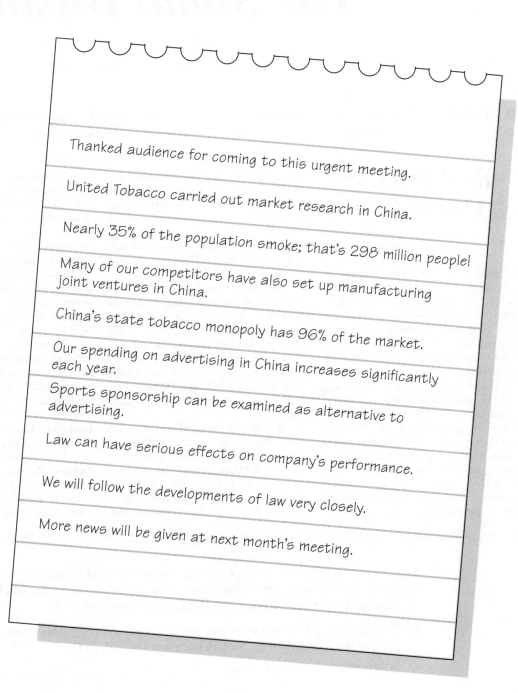

Thanked audience for coming to this urgent meeting.

United Tobacco carried out market research in China.

Nearly 35% of the population smoke; that's 298 million people!

Many of our competitors have also set up manufacturing joint ventures in China.

China's state tobacco monopoly has 96% of the market.

Our spending on advertising in China increases significantly each year.

Sports sponsorship can be examined as alternative to advertising.

Law can have serious effects on company's performance.

We will follow the developments of law very closely.

More news will be given at next month's meeting.

The Small Business

READING   Read the newspaper article below which describes the early years of Division Group PLC, a young British company, and answer the questions that follow.

Real Sales but Virtual Profit

By Erik Ipsen
International Herald Tribune

1 BRISTOL, England – What do you call a five-year-old company with 70 employees and £2.1 million ($3 million) in revenue for the first half of the year? In the virtual reality business, you call it the entrenched titan of the industry.

2 I guess that says this is a pretty small and new industry,' conceded Pierre duPont, marketing director of Division Group PLC, the fast-growing maker of hardware and software for virtual reality systems.

3 Five years ago Division consisted of four young men, all in their middle and late 20s, working out of a farmhouse in a town called Chipping Sodbury. Three of them had just left the big European semiconductor maker INMOS Ltd. and the fourth, Charles Grimsdale, had just left the British software house Perihelion.

4 All were well qualified as technology wizards, but only one had the slightest acquaintance with management. It was Mr Grimsdale's experience helping to manage his family's 450-acre dairy and cereals farm that made him the logical and unanimous choice as Division's managing director.

5 'We all felt stifled and wanted to do the things we wanted to do – things like computer graphics,' said Phil Atkin, one of the original gang of four and now Division's director of entertainment projects. Two years after its founding,

the company had grown to 18 employees, big enough to move into new quarters on two floors of a small building in a Bristol office park. Now that base has expanded to encompass two entire buildings.

6 It was an expansion fuelled in part by the company's first share issue, in May, which raised £5 million and valued the company at £13 million.

7 Six months later, Division is valued on paper at £33 million and its clients include companies ranging from Glaxo Holdings PLC in Britain to Matsushita Electric Industrial Co. of Japan and McDonnell Douglas Corp. in the United States. 'We have exceeded our expectations,' Mr Grimsdale said.

Now read the following sentences about Division Group PLC. Indicate below each one whether you think the information given accurately reflects the content of the article. If you think it does not, rewrite the sentence accordingly in the spaces provided.

1 Division Group PLC is a dynamic, new software company which was created six years ago by three of the founders of the British company INMOS Ltd.

❑ Accurate   ❑ Inaccurate ....

....

2 Figures concerning Division Group PLC's recent performance show that it is already making £2.1 million per year.

❑ Accurate   ❑ Inaccurate ....

....

3 The only thing that the founders of Division Group PLC had in common was the fact that they were all highly qualified in science.

❑ Accurate   ❑ Inaccurate ....

....

4 Of the original group of founders only one member had management experience.

❑ Accurate   ❑ Inaccurate ....

....

5 For the first two years the company operated from offices in Bristol and today it is still run from the same premises.

❑ Accurate   ❑ Inaccurate ....

....

6 Division Group PLC has now reached the stage where further expansion will be limited.

❑ Accurate   ❑ Inaccurate ....

....

7 Recently the company has been able to expand by selling shares on the Stock Market.

❑ Accurate   ❑ Inaccurate ....

....

8 Mr Grimsdale, an ex-employee of INMOS Ltd., is disappointed with the company's performance.

❑ Accurate   ❑ Inaccurate ....

....

VOCABULARY   1 Review the words from the key vocabulary section (page 106) as well as from the text (page 108) of the Students' Book. Use the words 'small business' and the clues provided to complete the grid below.

1 A .... trader is self-employed and entirely responsible for his or her business.
2 The opposite of 'part time' work.
3 The expenses involved in running a business.
4 Everything included; all totalled.
5 A shop that sells products made by a particular company.
6 Money owed; an obligation to pay money to someone else.
7 Machines, tools and other items needed to run a business.
8 A plan or project.
9 Ltd.
10 A business plan, often associated with the idea of risk.
11 To deal with.
12 A person or company that puts money into a business to make profit in the future.
13 Association of two or more people.

2 Circle the word that does not belong in each horizontal group. You may need to reread pages 106-108 of the Students' Book to help you.

1	interest	repayment	loan	shareholder
2	order	livery	artwork	design
3	partnership	company	venture	overheads
4	service	outlet	premises	branch
5	deliver	entrepreneur	customer	investor
6	consumption	capital	cost	finance
7	redundant	business	trade	turnover

LANGUAGE FOCUS

'Should have' and 'could have'

The director of a small business which produces notebook computers talks below about some of the mistakes that he made when he first started his company.

1 Each sentence gives an example of a mistake he made. Indicate, using *should(n't) have*, what better course of action might have been taken in each case.

1 Before starting my own business, I licensed the technology to another company which did not exploit it satisfactorily. I had to wait two years before being able to buy back the licences.

I shouldn't have licensed the technology to another company.

2 Our first notebook computer was not designed to be connected to other systems because we hadn't realised that our customers would prefer a compatible system.

....

3 We didn't spend enough time and energy on developing a strong dealer network and this affected sales.

....

4 At first we only targeted the individual consumer and it was only later that we switched towards the business users.

....

5 Marketing and advertising were our weak points. We thought that it was enough to engineer and design but soon learned that that was not the case.

....

2 Read each of the sentences below and match them with an appropriate phrase from the list (a-e) at the end. Then write a sentence using *could have* to show what alternative courses of action were open to this manager.

1 The capital of the company consisted entirely of bank loans and my own personal investment.

....

2 Initially our margins were too high and our pricing was unrealistic. We didn't realise this for some time.

....

3 When we got into financial difficulty at the end of the first year I didn't approach the public authorities.

....

4 My original team was composed of essentially older, highly qualified computer specialists.

....

5 Our offices were too big and on the west side of town where rents are the most expensive.

....

a This type of business can easily be run from a regional location.

b At that time there were a lot of talented, young university graduates coming onto the job market.

c I received offers from people who were prepared to buy into the company.

d It is sometimes possible to negotiate an agreement to defer payment of social charges and taxation for a short period.

e When we eventually did reduce prices this dramatically increased our sales.

WRITING You have recently heard about a Scottish venture to produce a new malt whisky, Isle of Arran Distillers Ltd. The company is inviting investors to purchase bonds (certificates) in exchange for which they will receive a certain quantity of the first whisky to be produced. You are interested in finding out more about this offer. Write a letter of enquiry to the company requesting information about the following points:

The whisky you will receive: description, date of production and delivery date.

▨ cost of bond: minimum/maximum investment, method of payment

▨ conditions: extra charges? VAT? customs duty? transport and storage charges? insurance?

▨ market price of whisky

▨ guarantee for your investment

Address:

1 The Cross

Mauchline

Ayrshire KA5 5AB

Scotland

International Trade

READING **1** Choose words from the following list to complete the passage below. You may need to reread the text on page 118 of the Students' Book. Use the plural form of the words where necessary.

entry	labour	opportunity
export	market	regulation
goods	measure	restriction
key	ministry	trading

In just forty years, Taiwan has become an economic giant. The [1]_____ to this success is the strength of its [2]_____ performance. It is now the world's 13th [3]_____ nation. The country's rapid development has come mainly from a very great number of industries requiring considerable amount of [4]_____ , such as textiles and footwear. The country's competitively priced [5]_____ can be found all over the world. This prosperity has improved the standard of living of many Taiwanese. Per capita GNP is now $10,566, the 25th highest in the world.

However, due to rapidly increasing land and labour costs, entrepreneurs are seeking [6]_____ in other Asian countries. Taiwan's government has therefore introduced [7]_____ to modernise its industries and to invest in advanced technology, such as computers and components. The [8]_____ of Economic Affairs is presently examining ways to attract foreign investors. Incentives are being offered to foreign corporations that will assist in the development of strategic industries. Banking and financial [9]_____ have undergone a thorough liberalisation and foreign banks can now set up branch offices in Taiwan. Some of the other advantages are Taiwan's location, its skilled workforce and abundant capital resources.

Taiwan's upcoming [10]_____ into GATT will increase its global perspectives, and already trade [11]_____ have been reduced: goods are now permitted to pass freely in and out of Taiwan.

Taiwan's main export [12]_____ are the United States ($23.4 billion), Hong Kong ($18.4 billion) and Japan ($8.9 billion), but exports to mainland China have been increasing steadily.

2 Decide if the following statements are true (T), false (F) or if the statement gives information that is not provided in the text (N).

1 Textiles and footwear are labour intensive industries. ....

2 Taiwan's gross domestic product is the 25th highest in the world. ....

3 Taiwan is trying to establish a new competitive advantage. ....

4 The government started its $300 billion development plan in 1991. ....

5 Taiwan has a strategic geographical position in Asia. ....

6 American banks cannot operate yet in Taiwan. ....

7 Taiwan has applied to join the United Nations. ....

VOCABULARY   Abbreviations

1 On page 116 of the Students' Book there are several abbreviations such as GATT, which stands for General Agreement on Tariffs and Trade.

Here are the full forms of some well-known abbreviations. In each example one word is missing. Find the missing words in the box below and complete the abbreviations in brackets by writing in the missing letters.

added	1 .... Delivery Date (–DD)
currency	2 Chief Executive .... (CE–)
deadline	3 Value .... Tax (V–T)
gross	4 European .... Unit (E–U)
important	5 Cost, ..., Freight (C–F)
insurance	6 Annual General .... (AG–)
letter	7 .... (of) Credit (–C)
meeting	8 Very .... Person (V–P)
fund	9 International Monetary .... (IM–)
officer	10 .... Domestic Product (–DP)

2 Now read the following sentences and definitions and indicate which abbreviation is being referred to in each.

1 Next week we are expecting a delegation of their most senior executives for preliminary discussions. ....

2 The project must be finished by the 25th of January. ....

3 She's been in charge of all aspects of the company's operations for two years now. ....

4 This is one way of measuring the wealth of a country. ....

5 The name for the association that aims to encourage financial co-operation between countries.

6 A percentage of the price of any item that is levied as tax.

7 A meeting of the directors and shareholders of a company held each year.

8 A means of arranging payment between a bank and a customer.

9 One of the terms used to describe conditions of shipment.

10 The common unit of money for countries in the European Union.

Commonly confused words

3 Look at the example taken from page 118 of the Students' Book:

Importers and exporters are constantly in contact, seeking his advice on the strawberry market … (line 15). *Advice* is a noun and should not be confused with the verb *advise*, which means to give advice.

Circle the correct word in brackets in each of the following sentences. You may need a dictionary to help you.

1 This report examines the *(relationship/relation)* between education and the level of development in Africa.

2 During the meeting, he made a brief *(illusion/allusion)* to the decline in exports to Western Europe.

3 Austria has been *(accepted/excepted)* into the European Union.

4 Of the two proposals put forward, I prefer the *(later/latter)*.

5 *(Who's/Whose)* responsible for consumer affairs in this company?

6 I've added an appointment with Mr Diaz to *(your/you're)* agenda.

7 The poor weather this summer will certainly *(effect/affect)* the grape harvest.

8 We attended a conference on the *(principles/principals)* of strategic management.

9 Our *(personal/personnel)* attend intensive language courses.

10 The company will *(adapt/adopt)* new measures to limit the number of goods which arrive damaged.

LANGUAGE FOCUS

Expressing obligation

Complete the sentences using *must, mustn't or don't/doesn't have to*.

1 A World Bank representative said that developed countries ___*must*___ continue to invest in the Third World in order to maintain standards of living there.

2 Stock analysts have made it clear that just because there are fears of a trade war between China and the US, this _____ interfere with trading on the Hong Kong Stock Exchange.

3 The US feels that China .... respect copyright and intellectual property laws before it can join the new World Trade Organisation.

4 You .... take that much cash with you on your trip; your credit card is accepted everywhere.

5 Merchant ships entering the UK .... be inspected as part of a safety crackdown by the Marine Safety Agency.

6 The company .... cut so many jobs; it hasn't examined other alternatives such as job-sharing.

7 The crisis that the African Development Bank is going through .... be left unresolved or else it will not be able to pursue its intra-African trade and investment projects.

8 We .... take the risk of investing in that country; the political situation is too unstable at the moment.

9 You .... fill in that form; customs doesn't require it any more.

10 More than two-thirds of shipments to Bulgaria .... be paid in advance.

WRITING The following graph represents Europe's contribution (% of overall total) to world exports over a twelve-year period. Write a brief description of the trends shown on the graph, using the expressions you studied on pages 122-124 of the Students' Book.

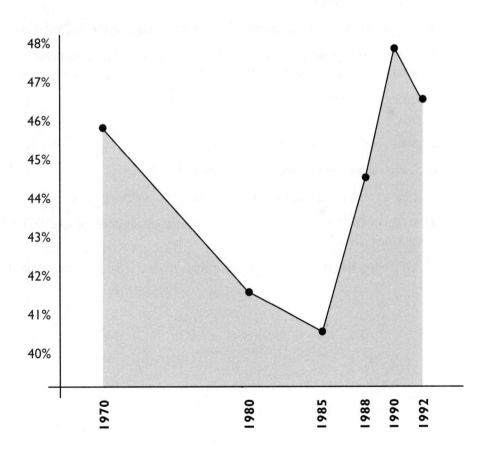

Insurance

READING

1 Brian Philips, a leading UK insurance specialist, is being interviewed about trends in the insurance market. The introductions to five of the questions are given here. Read these and then complete each one with a question from the list that follows.

1 In recent years some of the leading automobile manufacturers have been criticised for not doing enough to improve the security of their own vehicles by making them more difficult to steal.

....

2 In this country we've seen a significant increase in the number of car thefts and of thefts of car accessories. ....

3 Some commentators say that the re-insurance companies have too much influence over the insurance industry as a whole. ....

4 The Lloyd's market has undergone some major changes in the last few years. ....

5 Increasing uncertainty in some areas of insurance has led a number of advisers to suggest that the insurance companies should work more closely with their customers in order to improve their understanding of the risks they face. ....

a Which of these do you consider the most significant and why were they necessary?

b Do you agree that they are in too powerful a position?

c How is this affecting the premiums that motorists are being asked to pay?

d Do you think that this new approach will fundamentally alter the relationship between insurers and their clients?

e Do you feel that they should perhaps include more standard equipment on all their models?

2 Now read the answers that Brian Philips gives and match each one to the corresponding question opposite.

A In any industry which is losing huge sums of money something has to change, otherwise you'll go out of business. In this case we're talking about losses of £2-3 billion for the market as a whole! By far the most important development has been the decision to allow the institutions to enter the market with limited liability. This has both changed the rules and provided the necessary capital injection to allow the market to continue to operate.

B I don't really think that this is still true today. I mean, if you look at most of the models that are leaving the plants today you'll find that the majority are equipped with electronically coded security systems to immobilise the vehicle and these are pretty effective. In fact, I would say this is one of the reasons fewer cars are being stolen today than two or three years ago.

C Well, this has made life more difficult for everyone. The average car owner in this country, for example, is now paying almost double what he or she was paying seven years ago; and if you look at the figures, they are quite alarming. Last year alone almost 60,000 vehicles were stolen in the UK and 30% of those disappeared completely. Now that's a painful situation for both the insurance companies and their clients because it costs more money.

D This side of the business is not one that the general public is very familiar with because they only deal with the primary market. In fact, such companies are really acting as insurers to the smaller companies who don't have the resources to take certain risks and as such it is true that they do to some extent determine which risks can or cannot be insured against. In property, for example, some of them would refuse to cover damage due to terrorism.

E I think this is very definitely the direction that the industry will have to move in. It really covers a number of advantages for both sides because the clients will be able to receive advice and training which will enable them to operate more safely and, in turn, to pay lower premiums. The insurers will then be in a position to penalise those operations which do not manage their risks carefully enough.

VOCABULARY Review the words from the key vocabulary section (page 128) as well as the text (page 129) of the Students' Book. Use the clues provided below to complete the grid and find the key word.

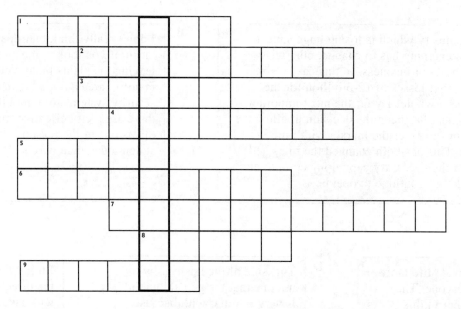

1 The amount of money that you pay to insure something.

2 A group of Lloyd's investors.

3 The dangers inherent in business and life.

4 The crime of entering someone's property and stealing their possessions.

5 Protection through insurance.

6 An estimate of the price of something.

7 Another word for a professional insurer.

8 A request for payment following an accident.

9 An intermediary between a client and an insurer.

LANGUAGE FOCUS **Countable and uncountable nouns**

In English there are a number of uncountable nouns which have no plural form, for example *information* and *cash*:

*Could you give me some **information** about motor insurance?*

*I haven't got any **cash**; can I pay by credit card?*

In each of the following sentences indicate with a tick (✔) or a cross(✗) whether the noun in italics has been used correctly. If not, write the sentence out correctly in the space provided.

1 The *informations* are in the brochure. .... ✗ ....

   The information is in the brochure.

2 Each *manager* has to complete an individual report. ....

   ....

3   Extensive *researches* were being carried out. ....

....

4   Insurance guarantees a minimum of *protections*. ....

....

5   The new *softwares* have been installed in the system. ....

....

6   Their *training* has been organised to cover basic communication skills. ....

....

7   Over the years our company has accumulated a lot of *experiences* in the field

   of laser scanning techniques. ....

....

8   Our *premises* are located in the centre of Brussels. ....

....

9   *Businesses* were especially good last quarter and this will affect our profits for the year. ....

....

10 The *datas* show a fall in the number of fatal accidents. ....

....

WRITING   You are the managing director a small company called Apollo Alarm Systems. One of your distributors has received a fax from the SRA, the insurance industry's technical laboratory. It states that several Apollo alarm systems (VIGIL 450, SAFEGUARD 563 and GEM SX9) no longer meet their standards and have therefore been removed from the list of approved alarms. You have called the SRA and they have denied all knowledge of such a fax. Write the fax that you would circulate to all your distributors informing them of the situation.

Apollo's address:

Apollo Ltd.

145 Milne Street

Coventry

Warwickshire

CV4 9JY

United Kingdom

Corporate Identity

READING   The multinational company BT, British Telecommunications PLC, offers a wide variety of high quality products and services (videophone, digital technology, mobile communications, voice messaging) to customers and business both in the UK and abroad.

Read the passage below which deals with BT's corporate communications policy, then answer the questions that follow.

At work in the community

As one of the UK's major companies and biggest employers, BT recognises that it has both the opportunity and responsibility to make a fitting contribution to the communities in which it conducts its business.

It does so with a comprehensive programme of support for:

People with Disabilities

BT supports projects that help break down the barriers which often surround people with disabilities.

A recent example is the launch of BT *Countryside for All*, a seven-year UK-wide project involving dozens of locally-based schemes and a national award scheme aimed at setting standards of access to the countryside for people with disabilities. BT is also a leading supporter of the British Paralympic Association and of the swimming programmes of the British Sports Association for the Disabled.

People in Need

Each year BT adopts a theme for its help for deprived members of society. The 1993/94 theme was homelessness, focusing particularly on the plight of young people.

Other areas on which attention is focused include HIV/AIDS education, empowerment of elderly people, caring in the community, and medical and health issues.

BT matches, pound for pound, employees' charitable donations through a *Give-As-You-*

Earn scheme which currently raises almost £1.7 million a year.

Economic Regeneration

Help is concentrated on job creation and training projects which benefit communities with significant economic or social problems. The formation of new small businesses is a key focus area including projects which help address the difficulties of rural communities. Training schemes are funded for groups of people who have particular problems finding work, such as the long-term unemployed, young offenders, people who have suffered from mental illness, women returners and ethnic minorities.

Education

BT's Education service develops partnerships with the education sector throughout the UK. Each year, more than 100 teachers accept placements with the company while around 3,000 students come for work experience. In-service training workshops are also run for teachers.

Major schemes of co-operation include the School Link Scheme with secondary schools and a Development Awards programme for universities.

Environment

Besides making sure that BT's own operations are environmentally friendly, BT also works to promote wider awareness of environmental issues.

It sponsors BT Environment Week, run in co-operation with the Civil Trust, and BT Environmental City to provide high environmental standards in urban areas.

Arts

BT is committed to providing the widest possible access to artistic talent. Tours of dance and theatrical companies and works of art are sponsored across the country to many towns normally too small to host major events. BT's sponsorship aims at stimulating innovation. A leading example is Northern Ballet Theatre, a lively young company which has staged a number of challengingly different productions.

In 1993/94, BT gave £15.2 million through its community programme.

1 Find words in the text to describe a person who:

    a has an incapacity or a handicap ....

    b aids a cause by approving or providing money ....

    c does not have a place to live ....

    d is approaching old age ....

    e does not have a job ....

    f has committed a crime ....

    g has gone back to work after a period of absence ....

2 How does BT work with its employees to help people in need?

....

....

3 For what types of communities does BT create jobs and organise training projects?

....

....

4 How does BT provide the widest possible access to the arts?

....

....

5 In what three ways does BT provide opportunities for those in education to gain an insight into its work?

....

....

6 In what other major area is BT concerned to create a good image?

....

....

VOCABULARY

1 Choose seven words from the following list of twelve to complete BT's 'vision and mission' statement. You may have to change the form of certain words.

conduct	focus	overseas
creation	network	requirement
contribution	match	project
growth	address	worldwide

BT's vision and mission

The company vision:

...to become the most successful [1] .... telecommunications group

BT's mission, its central purpose:

...to provide world-class telecommunications and information products and services

...to develop and exploit its [2] .... at home and [3] .... so that it can:

...meet the [4] .... of its customers

...sustain [5] .... in the earnings of the group on behalf of its shareholders

...make a fitting [6] .... to the communities in which it [7] .... its business

2 Now, using the remaining words from the list above and the information in the text on page 60, write five sentences about BT.

1 ....

2 ....

3 ....

4 ....

5 ....

LANGUAGE FOCUS

The article

Complete the following passage with the definite or indefinite article where necessary.

Deutsche Bank's Corporate Advertising

Deutsche Bank, [1] _the_ biggest bank in Germany, is running [2]............ series of 'courageous' advertisements in which people from many different professions and social classes express their views on [3]............ work and [4]............ society in [5]............ uncertain future. One of [6]............ reasons behind [7]............ campaign is that [8]............ bank is [9]............ shareholder and creditor of Metallgesselschaft, which made [10]............ heavy losses in 1994 on US oil futures trading. [11]............ banks in general have also been criticised for being inattentive to [12]............ customers' needs.

[13]............ campaign, designed by Abels & Grey agency in Düsseldorf, is not just [14]............ typical institutional campaign. It deals with [15]............ social themes and philosophical issues in a way that is very public and removed from its own business. It is [16]............ risk for the bank, but as [17]............ chairman Hilmar Kopper says, 'as one of [18]............ leading corporations of Germany, we are quite obviously in many social activities which go beyond [19]............ purely commercial' (i.e. support of [20]............ environmental research, help to [21]............ disabled, etc.). It is this 'other side' that [22]............ bank wants [23]............ public to know more about. In future, more companies may run similar advertisements, but they will await [24]............ response to Deutsche Bank's campaign first.

WRITING

As Marketing Director of the newly-formed London television station Capital TV, you are deciding which of three designs to choose for Capital's corporate mark. This will be used on all company communications, promotional items, etc. as well as on the TV screen. Write a memo to the designer, Lynn Fleming, stating which design you prefer and why.